A CourseGuide for

God's Glory Alone

David Vandrunen

ZONDERVAN
ACADEMIC

ZONDERVAN ACADEMIC

A CourseGuide for God's Glory Alone

Copyright © 2020 by Zondervan

Requests for information should be addressed to:
Zondervan, *3900 Sparks Dr. SE, Grand Rapids, Michigan 49546*

ISBN 978-0-310-11058-3 (softcover)

Printed in the United States of America

CONTENTS

Introduction

Welcome to *A CourseGuide for God's Glory Alone*. These guides were created for formal and informal students alike who want to engage deeper in biblical, theological, or ministry studies. We hope this guide will provide an opportunity for you to grow not only in your understanding, but also in your faith.

How to Use This Guide

This guide is meant to be used in conjunction with the book *God's Glory Alone — The Authority of Scripture* and its corresponding videos, *God's Glory Alone Video Lectures*. After you have read each chapter in the book and watched the accompanying video lesson, the materials in this guide will help you review and assess what you have learned. Application-oriented questions are included as well.

Each CourseGuide has been individually designed to best equip you in your studies, but in general, you can expect the following components. Most CourseGuides begin every chapter with a "You Should Know" section, which highlights key terminology, people, and facts to remember. This section serves as a helpful summary for directing your studies. Reflection questions, typically two to three per chapter, prompt you to summarize key points you've learned. Discussion questions invite you to an even deeper level of engagement. Finally, most chapters will end with a short quiz to test your retention. You can find the answer key to each quiz at the bottom of the page following it.

For Further Study

CourseGuides accompany books and videos from some of the world's top biblical and theological scholars. They may be used independently, or in small groups or classrooms, offering quality instruction to equip students for academic and ministry pursuits. If you would like to engage in further study with Zondervan's CourseGuides, the full lineup may be viewed online. After completing your studies with *A Course-Guide for God's Glory Alone*, we recommend moving on to *A CourseGuide for God's Word Alone* and *A CourseGuide for Christ Alone*.

CHAPTER 1

Soli Deo Gloria Among the Reformation *Solas*

You Should Know

- *Soli Deo gloria*: Glory to God alone

- The main points of debate between Romans Catholics and the Reformers: religious authority and the doctrine of salvation

- Rome claims that meritorious human works are accomplished by divine grace infused through sacraments.

- Luther sought to replace the theology of glory with the theology of the cross to explain how God manifests his glory to us.

- If God's glory implies humanity's debasement, is such a God really worthy of our praise?

- We cannot fully understand the glory of God without giving due weight to humanity's glorification in creation and especially in redemption.

- Central to John Hannah's work on God's glory are the moral implications of God's glory.

- John Piper suggests that "God is most glorified in us when we are most satisfied in him."

Essay Questions

Short

1. List and explain the five *solas* of the Reformation.

2. Explain briefly how the Reformers and Roman Catholics differed concerning the authority for the Christian faith and life.

3. Explain the Reformers' arguments against adding supplements to Christ's perfect word and work.

4. What was Luther's main objection against the theological method used by those who followed the theology of glory? Why did Luther say that the theology of glory was an exercise in human pretension or hubris?

5. Explain how human glorification leads to and supports the concept of *soli Deo gloria*.

6. Summarize Calvin's presentation that God is glorified through his creation.

Long

1. How does *soli Deo gloria* function as the glue that holds the other *solas* together?

2. By using philosophy as one of the methods in developing systematic theology today, are we turning back to a theology of glory that Luther criticized? Explain your answer.

Quiz

1. (T/F) The Reformers never sat down and adopted the five slogans of the *solas* as the official mottos of the Reformation movement.

2. (T/F) Grace is the ultimate standard of authority.

3. (T/F) Roman Catholic theology directly denounces the idea of glory to God alone.

4. (T/F) Martin Luther called for a theology of the cross to replace the theology of glory.

5. (T/F) Luther's theology of the cross and the Reformers' *soli Deo gloria* dealt with opposing issues.

6. (T/F) One objection against *soli Deo gloria* is that it seems to demean human beings.

7. (T/F) Different approaches to the *soli Deo gloria* motif in Scripture are the result of self-centered theologies.

8. (T/F) Johann Sebastian Bach demonstrated his pursuit of music for God's glory by appending "SDG" to scores that he composed.

9. Of what important truth(s) are we reminded of when we hold *soli Deo gloria* as the lifeblood of the *solas*?
   a) The religion captured by the Reformation is not about us
   b) The highest purpose of God's plan of salvation is not for our benefit
   c) God glorifies himself through the blessings he bestows upon us
   d) All of the above

10. What was the primary way in which God's glory is shown, according to Luther?
   a) Through Christ's miracles
   b) Through using reason to perceive God as he is in himself
   c) Through the humiliation of the suffering of the cross
   d) Through a theology of glory

CHAPTER 2

The Glorious God, Glorified Through Us: *Soli Deo Gloria* in Reformed Theology

You Should Know

- *Soli Deo gloria* has much to do with our Christian moral life, but biblical integrity demands that we first reckon with how the glory of God is truly about God.

- Reformed orthodoxy: a period beginning in the mid-to-later-sixteenth century and lasting until the early-to-mid-eighteenth century

- In Reformed orthodoxy, God's glory describes an aspect of his nature.

- Leigh states that ordinarily, God's glory is manifest in his word and works.

- Jonathan Edwards is the most well-known theologian in American history.

- Herman Bavinck and his *Reformed Dogmatics* reflects the general spirit of Reformed orthodoxy perhaps better than any other piece of theological literature.

- The Westminster Confession's emphasis upon the glory of God: God is all-glorious, and he glorifies himself in all his works

- An aspect of glorifying God that is NOT emphasized in the Westminster Confession: God enabling us to glorify him through our own conduct

Essay Questions

Short

1. What two perspectives do the Scriptures present for a biblical presentation of the glory of God?

2. What is the biblical story that presents *soli Deo gloria* in Leigh's theology?

3. Which perspective of God's glory did Edwards describe, but which Leigh gave little attention? What is the significance of this discrepancy between the two theologians?

4. What is the culmination of the expression of God's glory in Bavinck's perspective?

5. Describe the purposes of Christian confessions and catechisms.

6. Describe how *soli Deo gloria* is a fitting way to summarize the Westminster Confession.

Long

1. Which theologian discussed in this unit best presents your own explanation of God's glory? Explain your answer.

2. Do you agree with the Westminster Confession's presentation that God glorifies himself through superintending everything that happens in this world, including tragic events such as the Fall? Explain your answer.

Quiz

1. (T/F) While *soli Deo gloria* has much to do with our Christian moral life, biblical integrity demands that we first reckon with how the glory of God is truly about God himself.

2. (T/F) Richard Muller has provided much-needed criticism against Reformed orthodox theology.

3. (T/F) Edward Leigh claims that God's glory is part of him, but not expressed externally.

4. (T/F) Edwards failed to describe the Old Testament's use of the word "glory."

5. (T/F) Writing confessions and catechisms is one important way in which Reformed Christians have reflected on Christian faith and life as a task of the church as a body.

6. (T/F) The Shorter and Larger Westminster Catechisms begin with assertions that man's salvation is the main purpose of the Scriptures.

7. (T/F) According to the Westminster Confession, Adam and Eve's fall into sin was also done for God's glory.

8. In what way does VanDrunen suggest that a call for moral action, that Christians should pursue all activities for the glory of God as our supreme end, is somewhat imbalanced?

    a) God's glory concerns theological statements
    b) God's glory is something for us to meditate upon
    c) God's glory becomes centered on people
    d) The Reformers didn't view God's glory in this way

9. What aspect of God's glory does Leigh suggest is unknowable to any but God himself?

    a) God's internal glory
    b) The limitless nature of God's glory
    c) How God's glory is expressed in creation
    d) Why God demonstrates his glory

10. Which individual has emphasized Jonathan Edwards's key theme that God delights in his own glory in himself and in the happy state of his creatures to the extent that they reflect his own nature and beauty?

    a) Herman Bavinck
    b) Richard Muller
    c) Martin Luther
    d) John Piper

ANSWER KEY

1. T, 2. F, 3. F, 4. F, 5. T, 6. F, 7. T, 8. C, 9. A, 10. D

CHAPTER 3

In the Cloud: God's Glory Made Visible

You Should Know

- The events in the grand story of God's glory revealed in the order in which they appear: Creation of the World, Fall, History of Redemption, Incarnation of Christ, Crucifixion of Christ, Exaltation of the Messiah, Triumphant Return of Christ, Revelation of the New Creation

- The Old and New Testaments both use "glory" as a name for God.

- Jonathan Edwards's claims that "God's name and his glory, at least very often, signify the same thing in Scripture."

- God glorifies himself through judging his enemies.

- The cloud itself was a replica, a brilliant image of God's heavenly temple that is altogether invisible to our eyes (for now!). The nearness of the cloud meant the presence of God.

- Once the cloud descended into the Israelite camp and filled the tabernacle, even Moses was excluded from entering the tent of meeting.

- Scripture emphasizes the drawbacks and insufficiencies of God's revelation through the cloud. Distractors: persistence, accuracy, authority, sufficiencies, rewards

- Israel was guilty of treating the Lord with contempt when they exchanged the glory of the Lord for the image of a bull at Mount Sinai.

- The continual movement of the cloud contributed to a sense of uprootedness among the Israelites who traveled to the Promised Land.

- Monergistic: the work of God alone

Essay Questions

Short

1. What does Scripture indicate about God's nature when he is called by the names of King, God, or Father of Glory?

2. What is the first explicit way that the Scriptures describe God's glory and in what biblical book do we find this description first used?

3. How does the nearness of the cloud to Israel mean both the sign of blessing and threat of judgment at the same time?

4. In what way was the presence of the cloud a testament of God's love for Israel and a sign of his favor?

5. Describe the events surrounding the return of the cloud to the Israelites after the time of King David.

6. Explain how some of the prophets experienced the best displays of God's glory. What were the settings of their experiences? What did they see?

Long

1. Explain briefly how VanDrunen describes the larger story of Scripture as being the story of the revelation of God's glory. Do you agree with the suggestion that the story of Scripture is the story of the revelation of God's glory? Why or why not?

2. Provide a New Testament example of God's visible workings that strengthened the faith of the early Christians.

Quiz

1. (T/F) According to Reformed orthodox theology, the heart of the matter is that we are to glorify God in all our pursuits.

2. (T/F) God's glory is shown in his special revelation, his intervention in this world. His glory is not seen, however, in natural revelation.

3. (T/F) The book of Genesis never refers to God as glorious.

4. (T/F) According to the author's understanding of the pillar of cloud in the wilderness, it was like a brilliant fire surrounded by dense smoke.

5. (T/F) To be led, protected, and instructed by the cloud was to be led, protected, and instructed by Jesus Christ.

6. (T/F) Something greater than the cloud was necessary if God's glory was to be fully revealed and was truly to bless his people.

7. (T/F) Intimacy with God was only allowed for certain people at certain times when he appeared to his people in the midst of the cloud.

8. (T/F) The cloud of God's glory often brought curse as well as blessing.

9. Which of the following results is/are true concerning God revealing his glory in this world?

　　a) God's glory revealed in this world results in our praise to him
　　b) God's glory revealed in this world results in our service to him
　　c) God's glory revealed in this world results in further glory to God
　　d) All of the above

10. That glory is internal to God, being one of his attributes, is indicated in what way?

　　a) God created the world
　　b) God is holy
　　c) God's word is true
　　d) God is called God, King, and Father of Glory

11. Which passage is especially clear in demonstrating God glorifying himself through his sovereign power?

　　a) Ephesians 1
　　b) James 2

c) Hebrews 11

d) Psalm 119

12. What happened to the Israelites when the priests began ministering in the tabernacle?

a) Israel turned to idolatry

b) Israel trembled in fear more often than they rejoiced

c) Israel became more righteous

d) Israel began to interact more frequently with pagan nations

13. What is the effect when sinners' rebellion is confronted with God's glory?

a) Rebellion becomes more heinous and worthy of judgment

b) Sinners naturally turn to God

c) God's glory is diminished

d) God removes himself from the sinners' presence

14. What do the cherubim figures on the ark of the covenant symbolize?

a) The footstool of God

b) The angels that guard the way to the Garden of Eden

c) The angels watching over Israel

d) The angelic host surrounding God's heavenly throne

15. When does the glory of God visibly return to the Israelites?

a) When the ark of the covenant is returned to Israel

b) When David sees the glory in the tabernacle

c) When Solomon brings the ark into the temple

d) When the Israelites set up the tabernacle in Jerusalem

1. F, 2. F, 3. T, 4. T, 5. F, 6. T, 7. T, 8. T, 9. D, 10. D, 11. A, 12. B, 13. A, 14. D, 15. C

CHAPTER 4

The Brightness of His Father's Glory: The Glory of God Incarnate

You Should Know

- God constantly reminded the Israelites that their persistent sinful rebellion was incompatible with the blessed communion that the approach of the glorious cloud seemed to promise.

- God's own Son, "the radiance of God's glory," resolves the seemingly unsolvable problem of sin.

- The unique feature about the Old Testament prophets' message about the future of God's glory amongst his people is that God's glory would draw the nations of the world to its light.

- Isaiah 11 makes clear that the coming of the Messiah, David's son, corresponds to those other great future events we considered earlier.

- The temple is a symbol that best represents the Messiah as the One who reveals God's glory.

- It is a supreme paradox that the divine glory is manifest through humility.

- Jesus presents a contrast to the Israelites who would not obey God's will and hence were repelled by God's glory rather than exalted by it.

- In one sense Christ's earthly ministry is about suffering and his exaltation is about glory.

- Humiliation: the period between Christ's incarnation and his death and burial

- Exaltation: Christ's resurrection, ascension, and continuing reign at God's right hand

Essay Questions

Short

1. What hope for the glory of the Lord was given by the later Old Testament prophets? Explore and explain the imagery of this glory.

2. Explain what is unique to Jesus Christ as the true glory of God. Describe the ways in which Christ, after the cross and resurrection, is presented as the One through whom God supremely reveals his glory.

3. Explain why it is profound that Christ, the image of God's glory, shares in humanity's miserable condition.

4. In what way do the gospel writers maintain the paradox of glory-in-humility in recording the account of Jesus's transfiguration?

5. Describe the Trinitarian dynamic chronicled in John's gospel.

6. In what ways does the New Jerusalem fulfill that which the rebuilt temple in Jerusalem never could provide? Why is no temple needed in the New Jerusalem?

Long

1. The church is described in Ephesians as the temple where God dwells. How do you reconcile this with the Old Testament prophets' descriptions of an eschatological temple where God's glory dwells?

2. In what ways does glory to God through human suffering go against this world's view of glory?

Quiz

1. (T/F) Old Testament prophets foretold that the glory of God would return to his people in a rebuilt Jerusalem with its rebuilt temple.

2. (T/F) The coming glory of the Lord proclaimed by Haggai and Isaiah is for all nations.

3. (T/F) The temple proclaimed by the prophets found its primary fulfillment in the rebuilt temple following the return from exile.

4. (T/F) As the story of God's glory progresses, the attention shifts from the pillar of cloud and fire to the coming eschatological temple.

5. (T/F) It is striking and deeply important that the climactic revelation of God's glory took place in and through a human being.

6. (T/F) Jesus's first miracle does not show his glory, because he performed the miracle behind the scenes.

7. (T/F) Luke surrounds his description of Jesus's glory in the transfiguration with many reminders of his call to suffer, and of his followers' call to suffer with him.

8. (T/F) The Trinitarian God is glorified after Christ's crucifixion (and not before it).

9. (T/F) During Jesus's earthly ministry, his disciples apparently had no sense of the glory their Lord would someday enjoy.

10. What happened to the glory of the Lord at the end of the Old Testament time period? (p. 65–66)

    a) The glory of the Lord resided in the temple where the people could not approach it
    b) The glory of the Lord departed from the temple
    c) The glory of the Lord remained with the ark of the covenant
    d) The glory of the Lord went to Babylon with the exiles

11. In what way(s) is/are the New Testament glory different than the glory shown in the Old Testament? (p. 66)

    a) God's glory revealed in the New Testament is greater than in the Old Testament

b) The glory does not move around in a mobile cloud or is inaccessible to most in the temple
c) The glory is shown in the promised Messiah
d) All of the above

12. Which description(s) is/are true concerning Isaiah's statements about the return of Israel to Jerusalem following the exile? (p. 67)

a) God's glory will appear as a cloud of smoke and fire
b) God's glory will cover the entire city of Jerusalem
c) God's glory will be a protective canopy over Jerusalem
d) All of the above

13. What was/were the unique name(s) that Haggai mentioned of the One who would bring God's greater glory? (p. 69)

a) The One desired by all nations
b) Savior
c) The Holy One of Israel
d) All of the above

14. Which of the following items best explains the Trinitarian dynamic in John's gospel? (p. 76)

a) The Spirit glorifies the Father, who glorifies the Son
b) The Son obeys the Father, who sent the Son and the Spirit
c) The Spirit empowers the Son, who obeys the Father, who glorifies the Son
d) The Father sent the Son and the Spirt

15. What was the final chapter in the divine humiliation-then-glory story? (p. 79)

a) The resurrection of Christ
b) The disciples' missionary preaching
c) The judgment upon the angels
d) Christ being crowned with glory and honor to reign

ANSWER KEY
1. T, 2. T, 3. F, 4. F, 5. T, 6. F, 7. T, 8. F, 9. F, 10. B, 11. D, 12. D, 13. A, 14. C, 15. D

CHAPTER 5

The Glory of Christ in the Glorification of His People

You Should Know

- God reveals his glory in creation and through his people.

- In Jesus the glory of humanity is realized, and a redeemed host of fellow human beings will declare God's praise in the heavenly assembly.

- On the last day, Christ will return "to be glorified in his holy people and to be marveled at among all those who have believed" (2 Thessalonians 1:10).

- One of the great ways that God glorifies himself is by calling and enabling us, his people, to glorify him through our holy conduct.

- The specific way in which Scripture calls us to glorify God ought to provide important insight on the structure and priorities of the Christian life.

- God is glorified in faith because he is honored as the all-sufficient One who can meet every need.

- The worship of the heavenly temple and the worship of the earthly temple in some marvelous way were united.

- Until the time of the new creation, the people of God declare God's glory in worship in ways the Old Testament saints never experienced.

- Worship: a distinct activity of responding to God in prayer and song

- Doxology: a word of glory

Essay Questions

Short

1. Provide a brief summary of the revelation of God's glory from the Old Testament through the New Testament teachings.

2. Briefly explain the differences between glorification, justification, adoption, and sanctification.

3. Describe briefly what happens concerning our participation in Christ's glory when Christ returns. How is the resurrection of our bodies a central aspect of our glorification at Christ's coming?

4. Does VanDrunen seem to put glorifying God through our actions as the primary emphasis of God's glory or an extension of the glory that God expresses through various means? Explain your answer.

5. Describe VanDrunen's argument that to act in faith is to give glory to God.

6. Provide examples of the New Testament truth that Christians give glory to God in worship, in anticipation of Christ's return.

Long

1. What is your understanding of the gospel message? Does it include all of the benefits of salvation, and is ultimately about God's glory? Explain your answer.

2. In what ways can you expand your loving service toward others so that God may be glorified more thoroughly in your life?

Quiz

1. (T/F) All glory belongs to God, and yet Christians participate in the glory of God in Christ.

2. (T/F) To confess *soli Deo gloria* is to proclaim, in part, that God has worked such a great salvation in partnership with our efforts.

3. (T/F) God created human beings to reflect his glory.

4. (T/F) The gospel message is ultimately about the good news of forgiveness of sins through Jesus Christ.

5. (T/F) The completion of Christ's work meant the pouring forth of the Spirit, and hence also a greater glory than Israel of old experienced.

6. (T/F) Like their Lord, believers must walk through the valley of the shadow of death before they dwell in the house of the Lord forever.

7. (T/F) When doing all things for the glory of God becomes the principle focus, we run the risk of making *soli Deo gloria* primarily about us and our agendas.

8. (T/F) Nothing we do delights God more than calling upon his name with sincere hearts and declaring that all glory belongs to him.

9. (T/F) Because giving glory to God involves our entire lives, God does not take special delight in the distinct activity of worship.

10. (T/F) Old Testament declarations of glory to God often look beyond the narrow confines of Israel.

11. (T/F) The Old Testament provided for Israel to worship God, but discussion of worship by other nations appeared after Christ's first coming.

12. What has become the hallmark of sinful humanity in the footsteps of its father Adam? (p. 87)

  a) Self-glorification
  b) Pride
  c) Rebellion
  d) Judgment

13. Participation in Christ's glory comes through which of the following means? (92)

  a) Involvement in Christian ministry
  b) Participation in Christ's sufferings

c) Partaking in the Lord's Supper

d) Giving of ourselves to the poor

14. Paul makes the connection between faith and giving glory to God in which passage? (97)

a) Romans 3:23

b) Romans 4:20

c) 1 Corinthians 2:9

d) Ephesians 4:7

15. When does Isaiah suggest that all people will worship God and the whole world will be filled with God's glory?

a) On the day of final judgment

b) In the days of the Messiah

c) During the time of the new heavens and new earth

d) All of the above

1. T, 2. F, 3. T, 4. F, 5. T, 6. T, 7. T, 8. T, 9. F, 10. T, 11. F, 12. A, 13. B, 14. B, 15. D

CHAPTER 6

Prayer and Worship in an Age of Distraction

You Should Know

- Because our fundamental problem as human beings is our sinful hearts, no evil that seduces us today is brand new.

- There is at least one area of life in which focused attention and deep reflection are crucial for all Christians: worship and prayer.

- According to David VanDrunen, pious prayer that brings glory to God must be focused and it must be deep.

- One characteristic of the new technologies to consider is the way they foster a general culture of distraction.

- What we need to do is strive against the influences of contemporary culture by cultivating the virtues that promote godly prayer.

- Because we are often tempted to discouragement, boredom, and doubt in our worship, we must be patient while God performs our sanctification.

- For Christians discouraged by besetting sins and weak in the face of temptations, it is great comfort to know that God does not leave us to sanctify ourselves.

- Heidelberg Catechism: one of Reformed Christians' most beloved teaching tools

- Corporate worship: the formal worship we render as the church, the body of Christ's people

- Virtue: a positive character trait

Essay Questions

Short

1. What temptations and seductions do you think have an especially strong hold upon us as we strive to fulfill our chief calling, to glorify and enjoy God?

2. Why is an emphasis upon prayer so important in the Reformed tradition? What are two primary reasons why we should pray?

3. Describe Old and New Testament teaching concerning the importance of corporate worship.

4. Describe our role in the process of our sanctification.

5. What is the benefit upon your busy life for keeping a weekly Sabbath? (p. 125–126)

6. Describe in general terms what the Lord's Prayer teaches us about how to pray. Explain the place of God's glory in the Lord's Prayer.

Long

1. What is your attitude toward corporate worship? Do you place the same emphasis upon it that is found in the Old and New Testaments?

2. Which virtues in your life do you see diminishing as a result of the use of technology? What virtues do you strive to develop in your life? What is your strategy to develop these virtues?

Quiz

1. (T/F) New technologies tend to multiply distractions in our hearts and minds, promoting shallow thinking.

2. (T/F) Corporate worship is the most important form of worship because Scripture describes the worship of heaven as corporate in nature.

3. (T/F) Because of the emphasis upon corporate worship, private worship is not an important forum for glorifying God.

4. (T/F) As long as the content of a message remains the same, it really doesn't matter what medium communicates it.

5. (T/F) When we go online, we enter an environment that promotes cursory reading, hurried and distracted thinking, and superficial learning.

6. (T/F) Self-control is central to fostering the reflective thinking skills and deep engagement in learning that are so needed, individually and collectively, in the digital age.

7. (T/F) The most important way to grow in the virtues that encourage concentration and deep thinking is to ask God to shape our hearts in this direction.

8. (T/F) Even if we become people increasingly accustomed to the more superficial relationships sustained by email, texts, and Facebook, we are not in danger of losing our ability to cultivate our relationship with God.

9. (T/F) God is our sanctifier, who carries out this work in spite of our own battles against temptation.

10. (T/F) Practicing a weekly Sabbath provides time for unhurried worship and enhanced fellowship.

11. (T/F) The only prayer given specifically as a model and summary of godly prayer is the Lord's Prayer.

12. Why was it not possible for most of God's people in biblical times to read the Scriptures privately?
   a) They had no access to books before the days of modern publishing
   b) The Scriptures were in languages unfamiliar to them
   c) Only the priests could access the Scriptures
   d) The Jews would not allow the Gentiles into the synagogues

13. What is/are the most important part(s) of our gratitude toward God? (p. 111)
   a) Prayer
   b) Bible study

c) Evangelism

d) All of the above

14. Which of the following is NOT listed among the virtues that promote faithful prayer and worship?

a) Self-control

b) Patience

c) Meekness

d) Intimacy

15. What is an excellent place to develop worship-building virtues that avoid the problems of technology?

a) Spend quality conversation time with friends and family

b) Watch movies with friends and family

c) Spend time texting with friends and family

d) Write letters to friends and family

CHAPTER 7

The Fear of the Lord in an Age of Narcissism

You Should Know

- Christian moral theology has traditionally identified vainglory as one of the seven deadly vices, a vice to which every person is tempted.

- Fear of the Lord is a fundamental mark of true godliness that is directly contrary to narcissism. Christians tend not to fear the Lord because the Lord removes fear.

- We continue to fear God as we admire his infinitely perfect attributes that ought to "engender reverence" in us.

- The structure of the social networking sites rewards the skills of the narcissist, such as self-promotion, selecting flattering photographs of oneself, and having the most friends.

- A proper self-assessment depends greatly on the virtue of humility.

- Our awe for God is enhanced by knowing that the perfectly holy and just God forgives sins.

- Narcissism: an excessively high and unrealistic opinion about oneself and an obsession with one's public image

- Fear: 1) characterized by terror, "slavish"; 2) reverential awe, "filial"

- Vainglory: the excessive and disordered desire for recognition and approval from others

- Entitlement: the pervasive belief that one deserves special treatment, success, and more material things

Essay Questions

Short

1. Explain how narcissism is in competition with the concept of *soli Deo gloria*.

2. Explain the differences between "slavish fear" and "filial fear," and to whom these two kinds of fear pertain.

3. Do you agree with the suggestion that the glory of God spurs a reverential fear of the Lord in the godly heart, and that this reverential fear cannot help but spring forth into praise? Why or why not?

4. Explain how the vice of vainglory is antithetical to the theme of *soli Deo gloria*.

5. Provide a description of narcissists.

6. Explain why loving the truth about God and ourselves counters our narcissistic thinking.

Long

1. In what area of your life are you most susceptible to narcissism? How do you measure up against the description of narcissism? Do you have tendencies that need correction?

2. What is your sense of the fear of the Lord in your life? Is this a liberating or a restrictive doctrine for you? How do you suggest that we cultivate a healthy fear of the Lord and counter the allure of narcissism?

Quiz

1. (T/F) Fear of the Lord is the preeminent characteristic of the godly heart.

2. (T/F) The godly person does not need to shudder at the heinousness of sin and feel deep contrition before the face of an infinitely pure God, because of Christ.

3. (T/F) Christians fear God because the reverential awe with which we regard our God is precisely why the threats of all other foes recede from the eye of faith.

4. (T/F) The Old and New Testaments describe believers' reverence of God resulting in their worship of God.

5. (T/F) Our fear of the Lord will decrease in heaven, as we will be free from sin.

6. (T/F) It is impossible tro be a God-fearer and a narcissist at the same time.

7. (T/F) In the minds of narcissists, achievements are more important than impressions.

8. (T/F) Experts suggest that a narcissism epidemic began in the 1870s.

9. (T/F) For narcissists, material goods such as a Rolex watch, a luxury car, and a huge kitchen with granite countertops are signals of status.

10. (T/F) Cosmetic surgery in the United States increased three times between 1997 and 2007.

11. The lack of fear of the Lord may be the result of having what view of God?
   a) God is distant from us and unapproachable
   b) God is humanized and on our level
   c) God is a holy, righteous judge
   d) God is the King of all creation

12. What triggers the reverential fear of the Lord in the godly heart?
   a) The commands of Scripture
   b) The fear of God's judgment
   c) God's all-surpassing glory
   d) All of the above

13. Which statistic in 2006 suggests that vainglory in America has reached an epidemic proportion?
   a) 2 out of 5 Americans in their twenties have a gym membership
   b) 1 out of 5 Americans think they could be a movie star

    c) 1 out of 10 Americans in their twenties have symptoms of the Narcissistic Personality Disorder

    d) 4 out of 5 Americans take selfies

14. Which of the following messages are NOT instilled in young people through social networking:

    a) Avoid interaction with older generations

    b) The need for constant entertainment

    c) Flaunt it if you've got it

    d) Success through being a consumer

15. Which of the following is/are (a) practical way(s) to diminish the temptations of vanity and narcissism?

    a) Modify or restrict our use of social media

    b) Cut off various lines of credit

    c) Evaluate the self-centeredness messages we send to impressionable children

    d) All of the above

CHAPTER 8

Glorifying God in an Age That Is Passing

You Should Know

- When Scripture speaks of glorifying God in our life activities, it never associates it with a program of cultural transformation.

- This present age is one of vanity and presents dangers and temptations that Christians must shun.

- Peter's term for "sojourner" refers to people temporarily living in or traveling through a place that is not their true home.

- Some of the strongest biblical exhortations to self-denial are explained in light of the glory to come.

- He who has learned to look to God in everything he does, is at the same time diverted from all vain thoughts.

- "The age that is passing": the entire period in which the New Testament church has lived

- Civil, or common kingdom: a kingdom in which God upholds the activities and institutions of this world despite its fall into sin

- Spiritual, or redemptive kingdom: a kingdom in which God saves a people for himself, gathering them now into the church, and one day bringing them home to the new creation

- Patience: the believer's spiritual strength which he has in God whereby he endures all the vicissitudes of life, having a hope that the outcome will be well

- Christian joy: a deep-seated virtue of the heart, not a mood that waxes and wanes, that is a delight in God, in his good gifts, and in our vocation to serve him

Essay Questions

Short

1. Describe how Scripture speaks of this present age concerning glory. Describe the differences of the present and coming ages in terms of glory.

2. Explain the common kingdom view. Explain the spiritual or redemptive kingdom view.

3. Provide a brief explanation of what it means to glorify God in all that we do.

4. List some of the good purposes God has in bringing us to glory along the path of hardship and self-denial, according to Calvin. What does this mean for your life?

5. According to Calvin, what is the center upon which we learn to bear the cross in a life of self-denial?

6. Explain why patient endurance is intimately connected to hope. Explain why self-denial and patient endurance, although necessary, may suggest that the Christian life is simply one of grim resignation.

Long

1. In what ways does the concept of two ages help you to see the struggles we face and the hope that we have in order to face them?

2. Which part of setting your eyes upon God's glory, which entails a longing for the age to come and steadfastness in the face of present trials, is the most difficult for you? What changes can you make to improve in that area?

Quiz

1. (T/F) Glory is one of the characteristics that makes God who he is, and all of his characteristics are glorious.

2. (T/F) In Paul's presentation, the world in which we live is entirely and unambiguously evil.

3. (T/F) In the two kingdoms view, God rules them by different means, though for the same purposes.

4. (T/F) The "kingdom of God" is a spiritual kingdom in the sense that it is not an appendage to civil government.

5. (T/F) A sojourner and an exile differ, in that an exile does not live in his true home

6. (T/F) Glorifying God in this present age means, first of all, to render right worship to him, especially in the church's corporate assembly.

7. (T/F) Self-denial is about the last thing that comes naturally to us.

8. (T/F) Self-denial is another way of saying that we are to hate ourselves so that we can love God.

9. (T/F) At times John Calvin seems almost overwhelmed by the difficulty of forsaking one's own glory and other self-centered attainments of the present life.

10. (T/F) Self-denial is enhanced by, though does not require, patient endurance.

11. (T/F) As meditation on the future life sustains self-denial, so hope undergirds patience.

12. (T/F) The Scriptures emphasize that the difference between joy and happiness is that joy emerges through suffering, and even that we rejoice in suffering, while suffering does not make anyone happy.

13. (T/F) Courage pretends that there is no danger and acts accordingly.

14. Which of the following is/are not (a)main way(s) discussed in which God is glorified?
   a) Glorifying God through worship
   b) Glorifying God through the saints' holy conduct
   c) Glorifying God through glorifying his saints
   d) None of the above

15. What does it mean to wait upon the Lord?
   a) Do not make a decision until you hear a word from God through the Scriptures
   b) Self-denial, looking for the hope of glory, and actively serving God
   c) Spend extended hours in isolation and prayer
   d) All of the above

Notes

www.ingramcontent.com/pod-product-compliance
Lightning Source LLC
Chambersburg PA
CBHW011746020426
42331CB00014B/3302